Ahesh

<u>Eri</u>

International Women's Day

Nede [8][9]

Harriet Tubman Day

Breonna Taylor

Ruth Bader Ginsburg

Alel/Thabeshin I nede

One in three girls

and women

experience some form

of physical or sexual violence

in their lifetime.

Bath [18][19]

Ayaanin/Bath

Fifteen million adolescent girls

worldwide have experienced forced sex.

Nib [22][23]

Gloria Steinem

Every year, 13.5 million children

under 18 are married,

with many having

little to no say in the matter – and of that number,

12 million are girls.

Thab [26][27]

Ayaanin/Shinethab

Every three hours

a woman is killed

in South Africa.

Shinethab [30][31]

Athil

Ahesh/Nib

Boothab [1][2]

Women and girls together

account for 72 percent,

with girls representing more than

four child trafficking victims.

Bimethab [3][4]

Amahina/Thabeshin I Nib

Adult women account

for nearly half of all human trafficking

victims detected globally.

Bathethab [7][8]

Athesh/Budethab

A woman in South Africa

has a greater chance of being raped

than she does of learning how to read.

Adaletham/Nibethab

On average,

a woman is killed by a man

every three days.

Thabeshin [15][16]

Ahede/Thabeshin I um

62 percent of all

women killed by men

were killed by a current or former partner.

Thabeshin I shin [19][20]

Ayu/Nedethab

At least 34 percent of women

killed had children

under 18 years of age.

Thabeshin I bim [23][24]

Athon/Thabeshin I shan

Violence against women has become normalized in a world which more than 90,000 women are victims of femicide every year.

Thabeshin I bath [27][28]

Ahesh/Nede

Amahina

Around fifty-one percent of African women experience beatings from their husbands for going out without permission, arguing back or refusing to have sex.

Thabeshin I nib [1][2]

Ayaanin/Nedethab

In the last decade about 700 women have been killed

in Spain by their partners or ex-partners

in cases of violence against women.

Ayaanin/Thabeshin I um

Over 67 million women aged 20-24 years old

in 2010 had been married as girls.

Fifty percent in Asia, and one fifth in Africa.

Thabeboo I shin [9][10]

Florence Nightingale

In the remote north of Vietnam,

girls as young as thirteen are disappearing.

Over the past three years alone,

hundreds have gone missing.

Girls are being kidnapped by bride traffickers,

taken to China, and sold into marriage.

<u>Oom</u>

Adol/Boo

Globally,

thirty-five percent of women

have experienced physical and /or sexual intimate partner
violence,

or sexual violence by a non-partner.

Athesh/Shinethab

Mary Anning

Amada/Thabeshin I bath

Less than forty percent

of the women who experience

violence seek help of

any sort.

Thabebim [25][26]

Athesh/Thabeshin I boo

One in three girls

and women

experience some form

of physical or sexual violence

in their lifetime.

Thabebim I shin [29][30]

Athesh

Ayaanin/Nedethab

Many women are terrified

by these threats of violence

and this essentially influences

their lives so that they are impeded

to exercise their human rights.

Angelina Jolie

Women and girls dedicate roughly
12.5 billion hours to unpaid work
every day.

Adaletham/Bud

Women's unpaid care work

has a monetary value

of $10.8 trillion a year.

Ayu/Boothab

Bessie Coleman

Amada/Thabeboo I nede

International Day for the Elimination of sexual Violence in Conflict

Thabeshan I shin [18][19]

Patrice Cullors

Thabeshan I boo [20][21]

Forty-two percent

of women are excluded from the

labor market.

Adol/Thab

Not one single country has achieved gender parity.

Ayu/Shinethab

Amada

Few of us will see gender parity within our lifetimes.

Thabeshan I nib [1][2]

Henrietta Swan Leavitt

Gender parity will not be attained until almost a century later.

Thabebath [5][6]

Athon/Nibethab

Almost 90% of people (women and men) are biased against women.

Malala Yousafzai

Only 10% of men and 14% of women are free of bias against women.

Emmeline Pankhurst

Statistically, prejudice against women is not improving.

Amahina/Thabeshin I shan

Women with full-time jobs only earn about 77 percent of their male counterpart's earnings.

Dama

Amelia Earhart

Rosalind Franklin

Adaletham/Bath

Women around the world aged 15-44 are more at risk from
rape and domestic violence than from cancer, malaria, car
accidents and war.

Adaletham/Thabeshin I bath

More than 20 million women are refugees.

Ahede/Umethab

One in five women in U.S. college campuses have experienced sexual assault.

Thabebum I bath [6][7]

Ayu/Boothab

At least 1000 honor killings occur in India and Pakistan each annually.

Athon/boo

Globally, girls are being married off at a rate of 33,000 a day.

Thabenib [14][15]

Madonna Louise Ciccone

Globally, only 3 in every 10 adolescent girls and young women aged 15-24 have comprehensive and accurate knowledge of HIV.

Adol/Boo

62 million girls are denied education all over world.

Thabenib I bim [22][23]

Amada/Thabeshin I Bath

Women's Equality Day

Athesh/Shanethab

Every 90 seconds, a woman dies during pregnancy or child birth.

Thabenib I nib [29][30]

Alel/Bathethab

Most are preventable, but due to gender discrimination many women are not given the proper care or education they need.

Thabebud [2][3]

Beyoncé Giselle Knowles-Carter

Women account for seventy percent of the population in absolute poverty.

Thabebud I shin [6][7]

Ayaanin/Nedethab

603 million women live in countries where domestic violence
is not considered a crime.

Tarana Burke

Chimamamanda Ngozi Adichie

Ayaanin/Thabeshin I um

In India, around seventy percent are victims of domestic violence.

Ahesh/Nede

In Turkey, forty-two percent of women over 15 have suffered physical or sexual violence.

Gloria Jean Watkins

Between 950,000 and 3,000,000 incidents of domestic violence are reported in the U.S. each year.

Debe I shin [26][27]

Athon/Thabeshin I shan

Ayu

About 2.3 million people are raped or physically assaulted each year by a current or former intimate partner in the U.S.

Debe I bim [30][1]

Ohena

Ayu/Nedethab

Women age 24 and under suffer from the highest rates of
rape.

Debe I bath [4][5]

Aton/Boo

On average, nearly 20 people per minute are physically abused by an intimate partner in the United States.

Debe I nib [8][9]

International Day of the Girl child

Debe I bud [10][11]

Margaret Hilda Thatcher

International Rural Women Day

One in seven women have been injured by an intimate partner.

Adol/Boo

On a typical day, there are more than twenty thousand phone calls placed to domestic violence hotlines in the United States.

Ahesh/Nede

The presence of a fire arm in a domestic violence situation increases the risk of homicide by 500%.

Hillary Rodham Clinton

Less than 30% of people injured by intimate partners receive medical cares for their injuries.

Debe I Nibethab [28][29]

Ahede/Thabeshin I Um

Athon

One in seven women have been stalked by an intimate partner during their lifetime to the point in which they felt very fearful or believed that they or some one close to them would be harmed.

Adaletham/Nibethab

Domestic victimization is correlated with a higher rate of depression and suicidal behavior.

Debe I thabeshin I shin [5][6]

Marie Sklodowska Curie

Black women have to work nineteen months to make what white men did in a year.

Elizabeth Cady Stanton

Women make up more than two-thirds of world's population living in abject poverty.

Athesh/Budethab

It would take 135 years to close the gender gap in Africa.

Debe I thabeshin I nib [17][18]

Amahina/Thabeshin I nib

In North Africa, it would take 153 years to close the gender gap.

Aton/Boo

International Day for the Elimination of Violence against Women

Sojourner Truth

Debe I thabeboo I shin [25][26]

Adol/Boo

Widahoth

The gender gap in political appointment now requires another hundred years to be bridged.

Ayaanin/Shinethab

Girls from poor families are more than three times more
likely to marry before eighteen as girls from wealthier family.

Ayaanin/Bath

130 million girls are out of school.

Grace Brewster Murray Hopper

Half a billion women cannot read.

Alel/Thabeshin I nede

Equatorial Guinea, Sierra Leone, Tanzania, and Burundi expel pregnant girls from school.

Amada/Thabeshin I Bath

Globally, 340,000 girls and young women are infected with
HIV every year.

Athesh/Thabeshin I boo

Girls make up three out of four new infections among children aged 10-19 in sub-Saharan Africa.

Debe I thabebim I bath [23][24]

Ayaanin/Nedethab

A young woman in sub-Saharan Africa is twice likely to be infected with HIV than a young man her age.

Debe I thabebim I nib [27][28]

Adaletham/Bud

Alel

Globally, forty-four percent of girls aged 15-19 think a husband is entitled to beat a wife.

Debe I Thabeshan [1][2]

Ayu/Boothab

104 countries around the world have laws stopping women from doing certain jobs.

Amada/Thabeboo

Simone de Beauvior

Adol/Thab

In sub-Saharan Africa, women and girls spend roughly forty billion hours a year collecting water-the equivalent of a year's worth of labor by the entire workforce in France.

Debe I thabeshan I bath [13][14]

Ayu/Shinethab

Michelle LaVaughn Obama

Ahesh/Nede

Over one billion women do not have access to a bank account.

Debe I Thabebath [21][22]

Athon/Nibethab

Angela Yvonne Davis

Amahina/Thabeshin I shan

Oprah Gail Winfrey

Adaletham/Bath

Ninety-nine percent of all maternal deaths occur in developing countries.

Betty Friedan

International Day of Zero Tolerance for Female Genital Mutilation

Alice Walker

International Day of Women and Girls in Science

Adaletham/Thabeshin I bath

Anemia afflicts twice as many women as men.

Debe | thabebum | shin [14][15]

Ahede/Umethab

Audre Lorde

Ayu/Boothab

Nearly one in three women and girls are anemic.

Debe I thabebum I bath [22][23]

Ahesh/Nede

Seventy percent fewer mums could die in childbirth – if all girls had primary education.

Athon/Boo

Ahesh

66 percent fewer child marriages could happen globally – if all girls had a secondary education.

Adaletham/Thabeshan I bath

US$28 trillion could be generated- if all gender gaps in work and society were closed.

Debe I thabenib I shan [5][6]

Feminism

Is the radical

Notion that women are human beings

CHERIS KRAMARAE

Debe I thabenib I boo [7][8]